Margaret Rizza
Contemplative Choral Music

Margaret Rizza
Contemplative Choral Music

Kevin Mayhew

We hope you enjoy the music in this book. Further copies are available
from your local music shop or Christian bookshop.

In case of difficulty, please contact the publisher direct by writing to:

The Sales Department
KEVIN MAYHEW LTD
Buxhall
Stowmarket
Suffolk
IP14 3DJ

Phone 01449 737978
Fax 01449 737834
E-mail info@kevinmayhew.com

Please ask for our complete catalogue of outstanding Church Music.

First published in Great Britain in 1998 by Kevin Mayhew Ltd.

© Copyright 1998 Kevin Mayhew Ltd.

ISBN 1 84003 297 9
ISMN M 57004 492 4
Catalogue No: 1450117

0 1 2 3 4 5 6 7 8 9

Front cover photograph reproduced by courtesy of SuperStock Ltd, London.

Cover design by Angela Palfrey.

Printed and bound in Great Britain

FL = Fountain of life

Contents

The Music of Margaret Rizza

Fountain of Life

Margaret Rizza's first collection of twelve contemplative pieces. A new, distinctive sound.

1400147	Full Score
1450090	Vocal Score
1400148	Melody edition
1480040	Cassette
1490024	CD

Fire of Love

A second wonderful collection, infinitely flexible and deeply spiritual.

1400194	Full Score
1450114	Vocal Score
1400195	Melody edition
1480052	Cassette
1490036	CD

Mass of the Bread of Life

A setting for congregation, immensely melodic and easy to learn.

1450110	Full Score (including free cassette)

Contemplative Choral Music

The specifically choral settings from Margaret Rizza's two collections.

1450117	Full Score

Chants and Songs for Contemplative Worship

A collection of the congregation chants, more easily arranged and in keys suitable for corporate singing.

1450118	Full Score

JESUS, YOU ARE THE WAY

Text: Pamela Hayes
Music: Margaret Rizza

head has found its rest in the beat - ing in your breast.

Je - sus, this a - lone can be my prayer, your pierced heart o - pen there.

Soprano Solo or Full *mp*

Je - sus, you are the way that I can hear the word that's

All other voices *p*

Je - su, Je - su,

spo - ken e - ver near. Je - sus, you are the

Je - su, Je - su, Je - su,

way that I can see all the Fa - ther means to me.

Je - su, Je - su, Je - su,

Je - sus, you are the way I can be-gin to let the Spi - rit breathe with-

Je - su, Je - su, Je - su,

in. Je - sus, my wea-ry head has found its rest in the

Je - su, Je - su, Je - su,

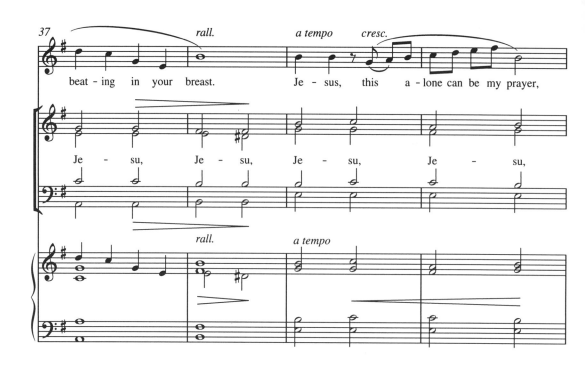

BASS CLEF INSTRUMENTS

YOU ARE THE CENTRE

Text and Music: Margaret Rizza

Pattern Guide

1. Introduction with C instrument to bar 20
2. Unison voices on theme to bar 20
3. C instrument variation to bar 20; voices tacet
4. SATB to bar 32 or all sing melody in unison
5. Instrumental variation; SATB (or unison) hum to bar 20. From bar 21 sing to the end using 2nd time bars

MIXED VOICES

You are the cen - tre, you are my life, you are the

cen - tre, O Lord, of my life. Come, Lord, and heal me,

Lord of my life, come, Lord, and teach me, Lord of my

life. You are the cen - tre, Lord, of my life.

Give me your Spi - rit and teach me your ways, give me your

1.

peace, Lord, and set me free. You are the cen - tre, Lord, of my

2.

D.C. *mp*

life. You are the cen - tre, you are my life,

mp

p rit. e dim. al fine

Fine

you are the cen - tre, O Lord, of my life.

p rit. e dim. al fine

INSTRUMENTAL PARTS

C INSTRUMENTS

Introduction ($\mathbf{\text{♩}} = 56$)
1: Theme

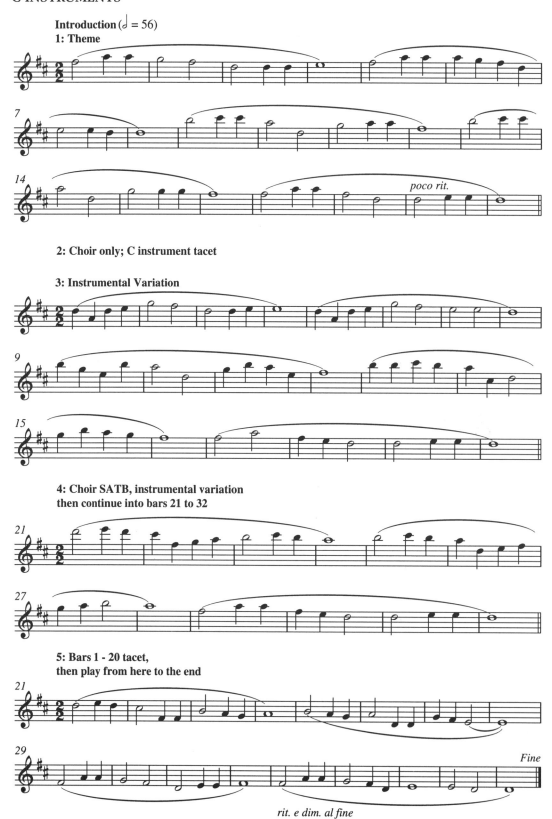

2: Choir only; C instrument tacet

3: Instrumental Variation

4: Choir SATB, instrumental variation
then continue into bars 21 to 32

5: Bars 1 - 20 tacet,
then play from here to the end

poco rit.

Fine

rit. e dim. al fine

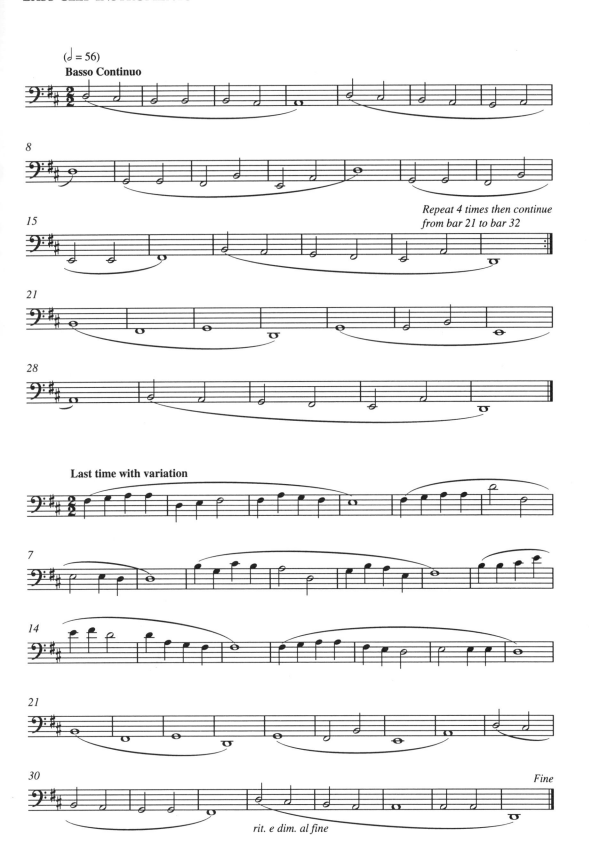

THE GRAIL PRAYER

Text: Traditional Prayer
Music: Margaret Rizza

Choir in unison

Lord

Je - sus, I give you my hands to do your work; I give you my feet to go your

way; I give you my eyes to see as you do; I give you my tongue to speak your

words; I give you my mind, Lord, that you may think in me; I give you my

spi - rit, that you may pray in me, that you may pray in me.

Soprano Solo or Semi-chorus

A-bove all, Lord, I give you my heart, that you may

Ah, *(or Hum)*

love in me your Fa - ther and all hu-man-kind; I give you my whole

(ah,)

self that you may grow in me, so that it is you, Lord Je - sus, who

(ah,)

live and work and pray in me; I give you my whole self, that you may

23

that you may pray in me; I give you my

(Hum)

heart, Lord, that you may love in me,

INSTRUMENTAL PARTS

C INSTRUMENTS

BASS CLEF INSTRUMENTS

* Bars in brackets are optional.

THE LORD IS MY LIGHT

Text: from Psalm 27
Music: Margaret Rizza

one thing I ask of the Lord: for this I long, to live in his house all the days of my life; to

Am Am⁷ Dm⁷ G⁷ Em⁷ C G⁷sus⁴ G

sa-vour the sweet-ness, the sweet-ness of the Lord; to be - hold his tem-ple; for this I long. The

Am Am⁷ Dm⁷ G⁷ Em⁷ C G⁷sus⁴ G

Lord is my light, my hope, my sal-va - tion; in him I trust, in him I trust. The

Am Am⁷ Dm⁷ G⁷ Em⁷ C G⁷sus⁴ G

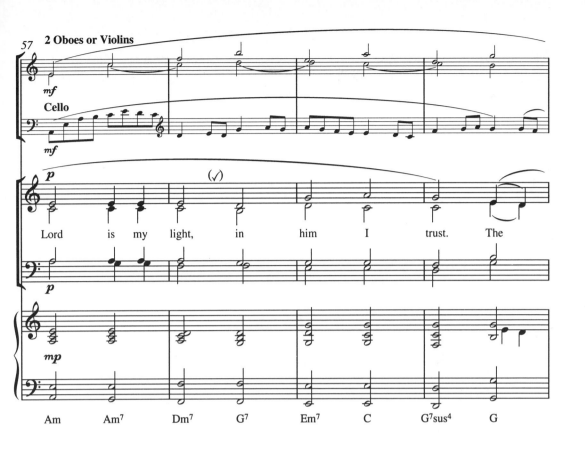

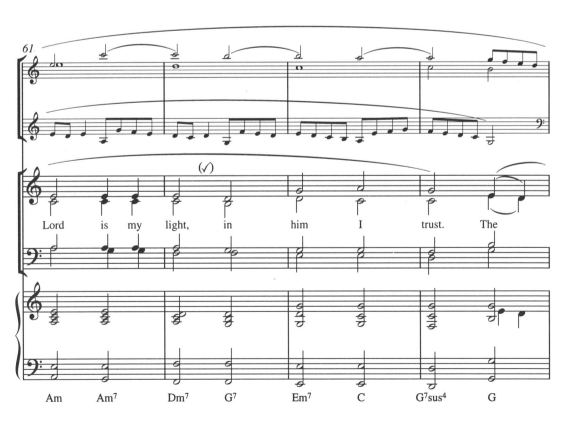

Lord is my light, in him I trust. The

Am   Am⁷   Dm⁷   G⁷   Em⁷   C   G⁷sus⁴   G

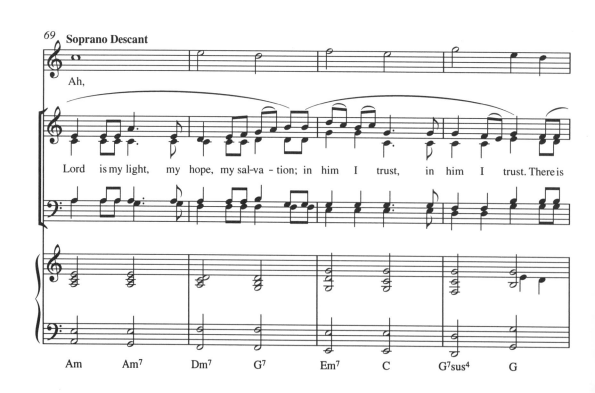

Soprano Descant

Ah,

Lord is my light, my hope, my sal-va-tion; in him I trust, in him I trust. There is

Am   Am⁷   Dm⁷   G⁷   Em⁷   C   G⁷sus⁴   G

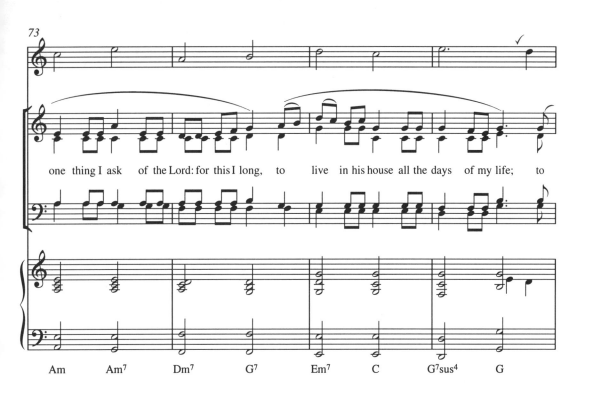

one thing I ask of the Lord: for this I long, to live in his house all the days of my life; to

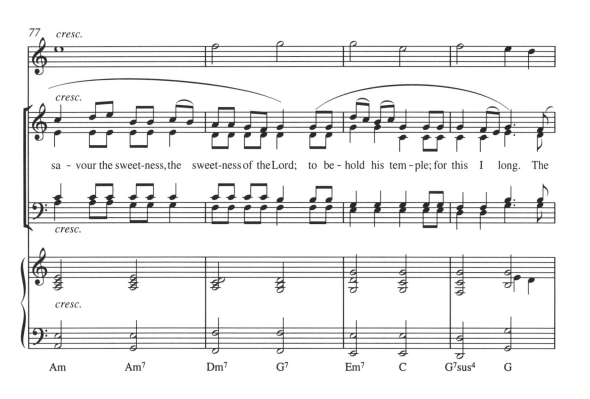

sa - vour the sweet-ness, the sweet-ness of the Lord; to be - hold his tem - ple; for this I long. The

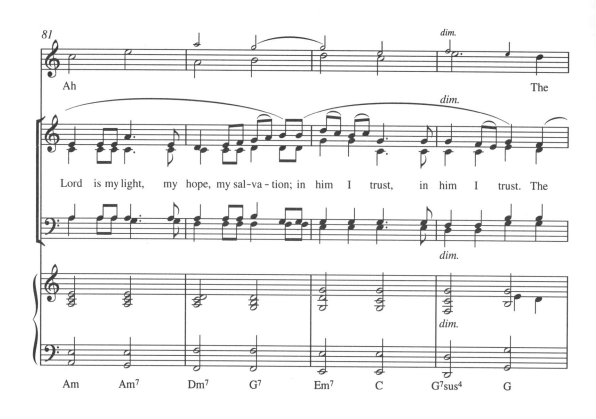

INSTRUMENTAL PARTS
C INSTRUMENTS

Larghetto ($\bullet$ = c.76-80)
Flute Introduction

Bb INSTRUMENT

BASS CLEF INSTRUMENTS

IN THE LORD IS MY JOY

Text and Music: Margaret Rizza

MIXED VOICES

Final Chant

In the Lord is my sal - va - tion.

dim. e rall. al fine

In the Lord is my sal - va - tion.

VOCAL VARIATIONS

Choral Accompaniment/Optional Introduction

Hum or 'Ah'

Soprano Descant

Ah,

ah.

INSTRUMENTAL PARTS

C INSTRUMENTS

Bb INSTRUMENTS

Eb INSTRUMENTS

BASS CLEF INSTRUMENTS

Variation 3

Cello I

Cello II

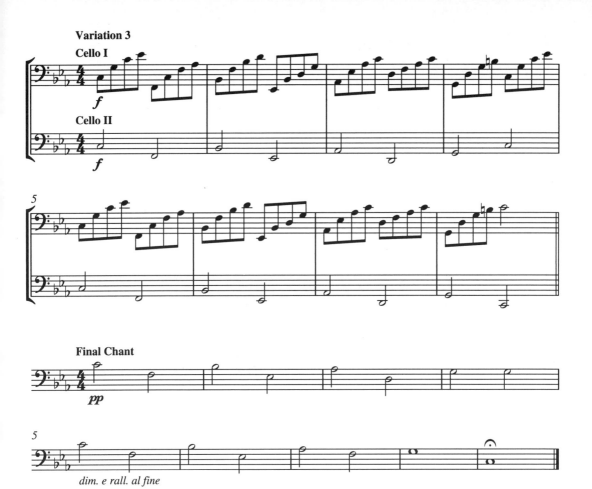

Final Chant

pp

dim. e rall. al fine

45

COME TO ME

Text: Matthew 11: 28-30
Music: Margaret Rizza

INSTRUMENTAL PARTS

C INSTRUMENTS

BASS CLEF INSTRUMENTS

ENFOLD ME IN YOUR LOVE

You are the light that is ever bright

Text and Music: Margaret Rizza

2. You are the beauty that fills my soul,
   you by your wound make me whole,
   you paid the price to redeem me from death;
   yours is the love that sustains every breath.
   O hold me, enfold me in your love.

   Optional harmony

3. You still the storms and the fear of night,
   you turn despair to delight,
   you feel the anguish and share in my tears,
   you give me hope from the depth of my fears.
   O hold me, enfold me in your love.

   Instrumental Interlude
   Unison

4. You are the word, full of life and truth,
   you guide my feet since my youth,
   you are my refuge, my firm cornerstone;
   you I will worship and honour alone.
   O hold me, enfold me in your love.

5. You have restored me and pardoned sin,
   you give me strength from within,
   you called me forth and my life you made new.
   Love is the binding that holds me to you.
   O hold me, enfold me in your love.

   Optional harmony

6. You are the way, you are truth and life,
   you keep me safe in the strife.
   You give me love I cannot comprehend,
   you guide the way to a life without end.
   O hold me, enfold me in your love.

see overleaf for mixed voices

3. You still the storms and the fear of night, you turn de-spair to de - light,
6. You are the way, you are truth and life, you keep me safe in the strife.

you feel the an - guish and share in my tears, you give me hope from the
You give me love I can - not com-pre-hend, you guide the way to a

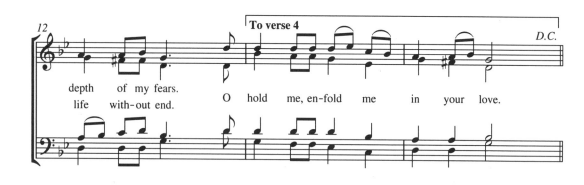

To verse 4

D.C.

depth of my fears. O hold me, en-fold me in your love.
life with-out end.

Last time

rall. *ten.*

hold me, en-fold me in your love, O hold me, en-fold me e - ver - more.

ten.

INSTRUMENTAL PARTS

C INSTRUMENTS

See overleaf for Oboe variation with verse 6 and bass clef part.

Variation with verse 6

Oboe

BASS CLEF INSTRUMENT

($\bullet$ = 84)

Introduction and Interlude   𝄋 **Verse**

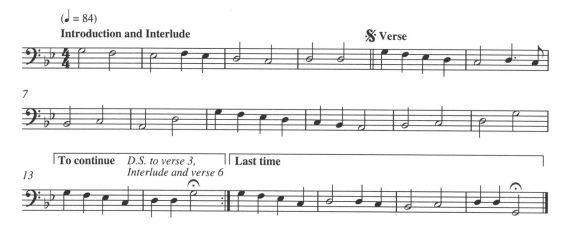

To continue   *D.S. to verse 3,*   Last time
              Interlude and verse 6

FIRE OF LOVE

Text: adapted from St John of the Cross by Margaret Rizza
Music: Margaret Rizza

*Based on the poem
'Living Flame of Love'*

fire of love, fire, fire, fire of love.

Soprano Solo (or Full)

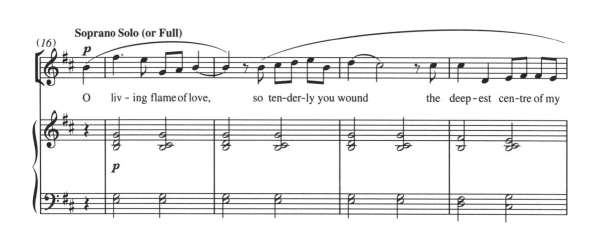

O liv-ing flame of love, so ten-der-ly you wound the deep-est cen-tre of my

soul, no long-er you op-press me, no long-er you af-flict me; now, if it be your

touch, that tastes of life e-ter - nal, life e-ter - nal, all debts are paid;

slay - ing, you changed death in - to life, slay - ing, you changed death in-to this fire of love.

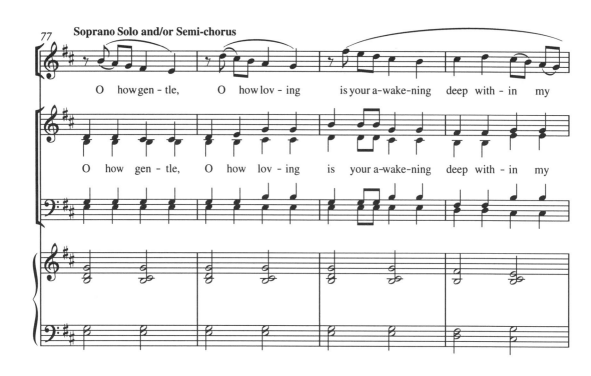

Soprano Solo and/or Semi-chorus

O how gen-tle, O how lov-ing is your a-wake-ning deep with-in my

O how gen-tle, O how lov-ing is your a-wake-ning deep with-in my

heart. There se-cret-ly you dwell, hid-den and a-lone, breath-ing the sweet-ness of your

heart. There se-cret-ly you dwell, hid-den and a-lone, breath-ing the sweet-ness of your

love, en-kin-dled in your liv-ing flame, O how ten-der-ly you rouse me to love you.

love, en-kin-dled in your liv-ing flame, O how ten-der-ly you rouse me to love you.

p veiled, mysteriously

pp veiled, mysteriously

Fire of love, fire of love, fire of love, fire of love,

pp

pp

fire of love, fire of love, fire of love, fire of love,

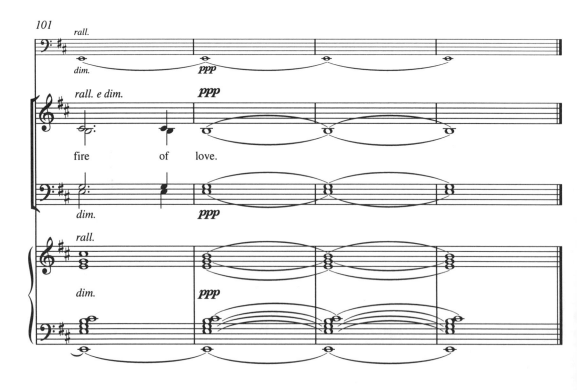

rall. e dim.

fire of love.

INSTRUMENTAL PARTS
C INSTRUMENTS

BASS CLEF INSTRUMENTS

71

COME, LORD

Text and Music: Margaret Rizza

Help us to serve and to love one a-no-ther, help us to turn and ac-cept the life e-ter-nal. Come, Lord, come to your peo-ple, u-nite us, re-con-cile us in your love. Come, Lord,

Optional accompaniment

Unison

come to your peo - ple, you are the light in our dark - ness.

Come, Lord, give to us your peace,

Come, Lord, give us peace, come to our war - torn, bro - ken world.

Come, Lord, come, Lord, give us your life, your life e - ter - nal,

INSTRUMENTAL PARTS

C INSTRUMENTS

Flute or Violin

FOUNTAIN OF LIFE

Text: Michael Forster
Music: Margaret Rizza

in - fi - nite grace, un - al - tered by time, un - hin - dered by space. Im -

in - fi - nite grace, un - al - tered by time, un - hin - dered by space.

mor - tal well - spring of ho - li - ness and peace; e -

ter - nal, in - fi - nite love with - out cease.

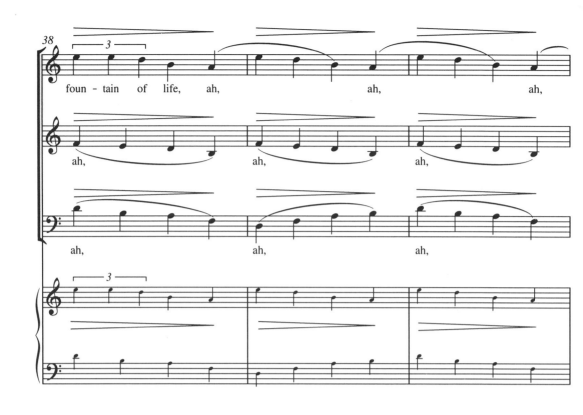

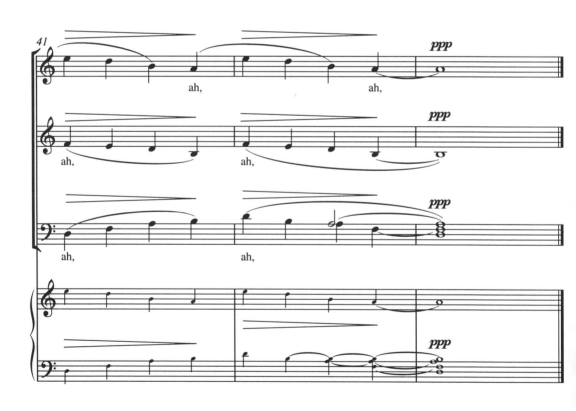

BASS CLEF INSTRUMENTS

83

TAKE MY LIFE, LORD

Text and Music: Margaret Rizza

1: Solo
2: Choir, unison

Take my hands, Lord, to share   in your   la - bours;   take my

1: Men, unison, on melody
2: SATB

Give me some-one to feed when I'm hun-gry, when I'm thirs-ty give wa-ter for their

Cmaj7　Am7　Dm7　Cmaj7　Am7

1: Women, unison, on melody
2: SATB

rit.

thirst; when I stand in need of ten - der-ness give me

Dm7　G7　Am　Dm7　Em　Am7

rit.

a tempo

1.　**2.**

some - one to hold who longs for love. love.

a tempo

Em　Fmaj7　G7sus4　Cmaj7　Cmaj7

33 **Cello**

Cmaj⁷ Am⁷ Dm⁷ Cmaj⁷ Am⁷ Dm⁷ E⁷

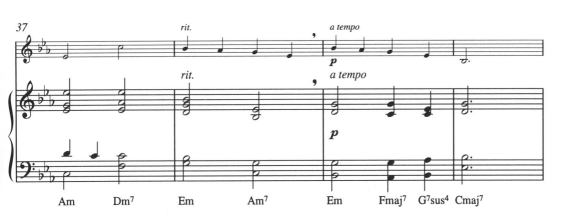

37

rit.   *a tempo*   *p*

rit.   *a tempo*   *p*

Am Dm⁷ Em Am⁷ Em Fmaj⁷ G⁷sus⁴ Cmaj⁷

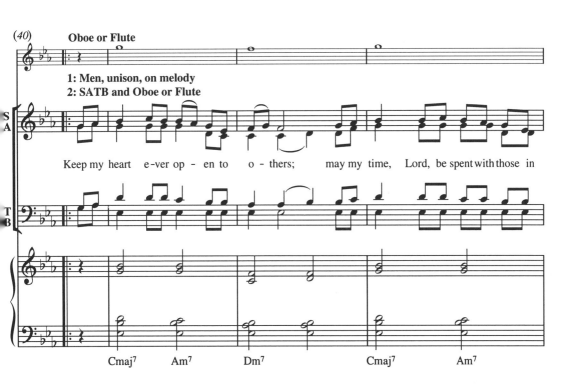

(40) **Oboe or Flute**

1: Men, unison, on melody
2: SATB and Oboe or Flute

S
A

Keep my heart e-ver op-en to o-thers;   may my time, Lord, be spent with those in

T
B

Cmaj⁷ Am⁷ Dm⁷ Cmaj⁷ Am⁷

87

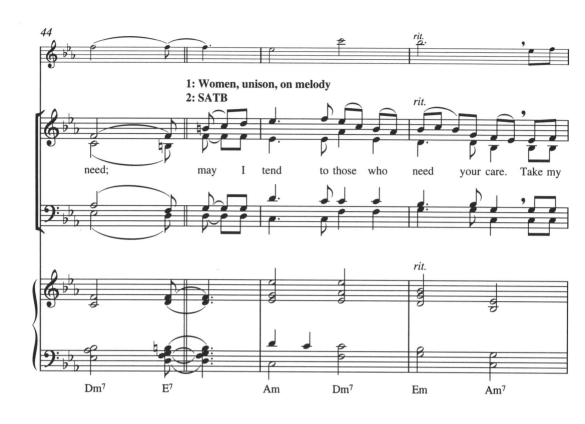

1: Women, unison, on melody
2: SATB

need; may I tend to those who need your care. Take my

Dm⁷   E⁷   Am   Dm⁷   Em   Am⁷

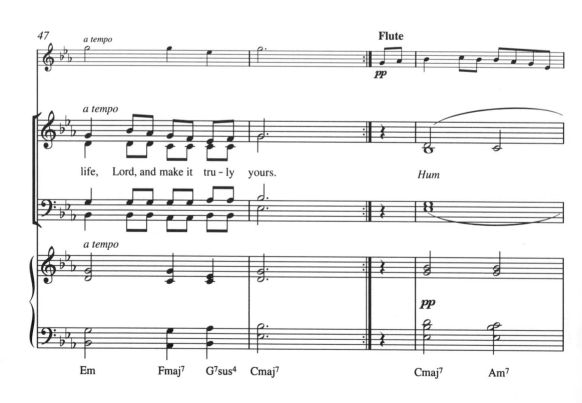

a tempo

Flute

life, Lord, and make it tru‑ly yours.

Hum

Em   Fmaj⁷   G⁷sus⁴   Cmaj⁷   Cmaj⁷   Am⁷

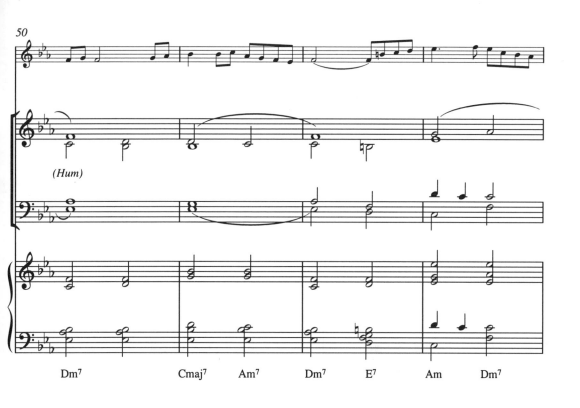

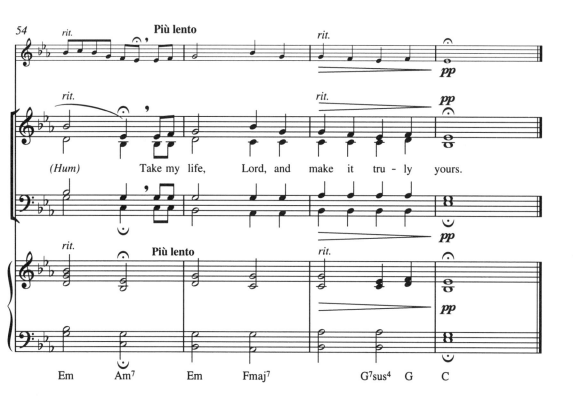

INSTRUMENTAL PARTS

C INSTRUMENTS

BASS CLEF INSTRUMENTS

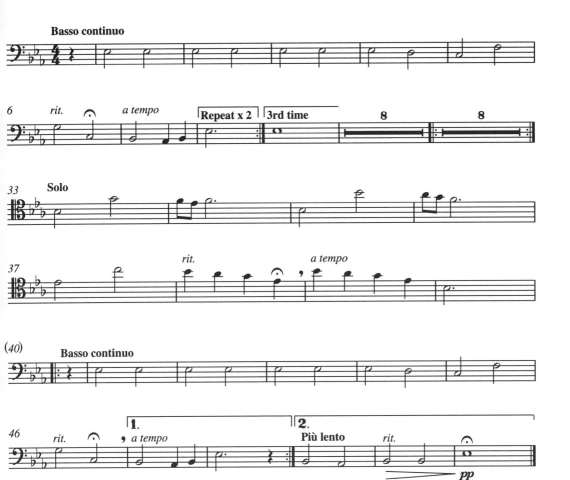

A BLESSING

Text: Gaelic Blessing, adapted by Margaret Rizza
Music: Margaret Rizza

MIXED VOICES

May the Lord bless you, may the Lord pro-tect you and

guide you, may his strength up-hold you, his light shine up -

on you, his peace sur-round you, his love en - fold you.

VOCAL VARIATIONS

Choral Accompaniment

'Ah' or Hum

Soprano Descant (with Choral accompaniment)

Ah,

ah,

ah,

INSTRUMENTAL PARTS

C INSTRUMENTS

See overleaf for E♭ variation and bass clef part.